HOW TO PLAY THE
HARMONICA
for FUN and PROFIT

by
HAL LEIGHTON

"The Original Harmonica Rascal"

1979 EDITION

Published by
Melvin Powers
WILSHIRE BOOK COMPANY
12015 Sherman Road
No. Hollywood, California 91605
Telephone: (213) 875-1711

Library of Congress Catalog Card No. 68-25646
ISBN 0-87980-213-8

Printed in the United States of America

TABLE OF CONTENTS

PART TWO

Trick Effects

PART THREE

The 10 Hole Chromatic Harmonica

PART FOUR

The 12 Hole Chromatic Harmonica

DEDICATION

To all the members of that broad fraternity
of music lovers, of all ages in every part of the
world, who derive education, enjoyment and
entertainment from the Harmonica, this book
is affectionately dedicated.

INTRODUCTION

**The Internationally Approved
Hal Leighton System
of
Harmonica Playing and Technique**

The Magic Numbers

Absolutely astonishing are the musical effects achieved on the Harmonica by Hal Leighton, foremost authority on every phase of this instrument. Those who have been privileged to see and hear him perform always ask the same question. "Is it difficult to learn how to play?" The answer is a very definite "No!" The Harmonica is a very simple instrument. He also adds, "Half of the world plays the Harmonica and the other half wants to learn how to play."

Many people can play tunes in as short a time as five minutes after first trying to do so. Naturally, as with any other musical instrument, diligent practice leads to greater proficiency and skill.

No special musical knowledge, nor previous musical training, is necessary because at the start the beginner follows a specially devised and now internationally recognized "NUMBERS SYSTEM" originated and developed by Hal Leighton, for use in training the orchestra, known as the "Harmonica Rascals."

Questioned about the method employed in selecting players, the author says, "The most important requisite in selecting players for any orchestra is that they are able to correctly hum or whistle a tune." In time all of "THE RASCALS" learned to read music at sight and to play with great facility from legitimate musical scores.

Reliance upon memory and the sense of hearing alone for accuracy is not satisfactory in many respects. The memory method, although a natural one for those untutored in the legitimate reading of music, is not altogether dependable. In group playing it is seldom possible to find a number of people all similarly gifted with retentive memories of equal power, and an identical sense of timing and rhythm.

Some simple, graphic method is needed to preserve with absolute accuracy, for future repetition, the harmonies, effects, and complicated arrangements essential to the proper rendition of distinctive Harmonica Music. With this in mind the internationally accepted "By-The-Numbers" System, was created and developed over a period of many years of practical experience by Hal Leighton.

THE HARMONICA'S PLACE
IN THE WORLD OF MUSIC

The enjoyment of music is the birthright of every one. It is natural for all children and adults to love music. Thousands of boys and girls never really learn to know and appreciate good music. Many who are musically gifted are unable to develop their talent for lack of competent instruction.

It is the aim and purpose of this book to assist all who wish to learn, in as simple a manner as possible, the correct method of playing the Harmonica. The unique versatility of the Harmonica permits its use either for solo or for group playing. The new, improved models, with their wide musical range and pure, cello-like tones, permit the playing of both classical and popular music equally as well. Finally the Harmonica is favored because it is practical, convenient and inexpensive. It is an instrument of unlimited and fascinating possibilities.

In progressive steps, you will see how very simple it is to learn to play the Harmonica. The text is easy to read and to follow. The liberal use of diagrams and other illustrations is designed to give all students an immediate, working knowledge of its use.

HARMONICA PLAYERS
ALWAYS IN DEMAND

Once you have learned to play the Harmonica, you will never be lonely again. You will always be in demand for parties, community entertainments, church and club affairs. If you "graduate" from the amateur or hobbyist classification into that of a polished professional, there will be no limit to the opportunities for the use of your talent. Motion Pictures and Television use Harmonica music for background themes. Night - clubs, Cruise Ships, Radio and the Concert stage are just a few of the media that use outstanding Harmonica players, both as soloists and as groups.

Just to repeat, the Harmonica is the least expensive and easiest, authentic, musical instrument to "carry" from place to place. To paraphrase a recent article, printed in an internationally famous magazine, never underestimate the power and magic of the Harmonica. More world-famous people have played the Harmonica in more unusual places than there is room to report. Among them, Astronaut Walter Schirra, who "smuggled" a Harmonica aboard Gemini VI, gave us the very first music from the vastness of outer space. Later on in this book you will learn, how to "Build Your Image as a Performer."

PART ONE

Simple 10 Hole Harmonica

10 HOLE HARMONICA

NATURAL SIZE

GETTING ACQUAINTED
WITH THE MECHANICS
OF THE HARMONICA

The regular 10 - hole diatonic Harmonica is built on a hardwood block partitioned into 10 equally spaced air chambers. Over this wood block are fitted two oblong brass plates upon which are mounted the small brass reeds which actually produce the musical notes. One plate contains the BLOW notes which respond when the player breathes INTO the instrument; the other plate holds the DRAW notes which respond when air is drawn OUT of the Harmonica.

The outside metal cover plates serve, not only to protect the delicately tuned reeds in vibration while the instrument is being played, but also help to complete the tone chamber from which the sounds come.

You will observe that the simple 10-hole diatonic Harmonica contains 20 reeds or notes - (10 BLOW notes and 10 DRAW notes) - set in numbered sequence, the low notes to the left and the high notes to the right.

So sensitive is the tuning of these reeds that very little breath is required to start them vibrating. The notes respond immediately. Because of this you are cautioned against loud playing which puts excessive strain on the reeds.

CARE OF THE HARMONICA

Lengthening the "Life"
of Your Harmonica

The Harmonica is in reality a very delicate instrument and should be treated as such. Try to cultivate an even tone (without stressing any particular note too much) whether or not you are "BLUE-ING" the notes. Try to remain relaxed while you are playing. Observe the work of the professional and you will notice how effortless his performance appears.

You will eventually select a favorite Harmonica on which to play solos. Your preference may be determined by which instrument "responds" better to your technique. You will acquire the "feel" of this particular instrument and automatically "sense" just how much air to BLOW into each note. Not too little nor too much.

Never STRAIN the Harmonica reeds. There is a definite limit to the volume of sound you can obtain from your instrument. If a note "sticks" or otherwise "fails" to respond, let your Harmonica "rest" for a time. Strike it "sharply" against the palm of your hand HOLE side down. See illustration of Page 51. If the leather valves have clogged or are stuck to the reeds, this process will "free" them. As moisture is usually the cause of "sticking" be sure to keep your Harmonica DRY ! Harmonicas are assembled and tuned by experts and

are delicately adjusted. If yours develops a
MAJOR problem don't try to fix it unless you
know exactly what to do.

Sometimes a reed will fail to respond because
of dust or dirt lodged between the reed and
the reed plate. This is a minor problem which
you can handle in one or two of the following
ways. Try removing the dirt, with a fine-
edged knife, without bending the reed out of
shape or disturbing its fine alignment. If this
does not work try "blowing out" the dust or
dirt with an atomizer, an empty one of course.

From experience you will learn to play with a
"dry mouth". The professional Harmonica
player develops this and performs this way
naturally. Until you MASTER this art, moisture will form deposits on the reeds or mouth-
piece unless you promptly remove it (the
moisture) by tapping your Harmonica slightly,

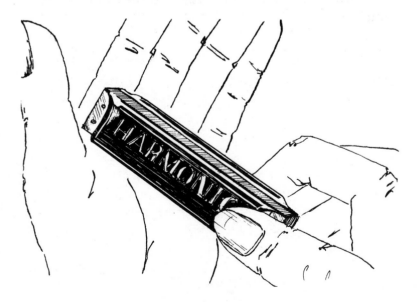

HOLE side down, against your palm. Wipe the cover plates clean with a dry cloth. For best results you should have two Harmonicas. This permits you to "rest" each one alternately.

Keep your instruments covered at all times when you are not playing them, whether or not you put them in your pocket. This will prevent dust or dirt from entering the air chambers and clogging the reed openings. Remember, once you play a Harmonica it is YOURS and it is not advisable to "SWAP" or "USE" one that anyone else has played. This, obviously, is recommended for sanitary and health reasons. You will find that having two Harmonicas is a worthwhile investment and, in the long run, both will last longer.

Moisture in the air, on foggy or rainy days, will effect the reeds and leathers. On days like these, dry your Harmonica more frequently.

LESSON ONE

Which Harmonica and Why?

The first question usually asked by the new
student of the Harmonica is, "With what Harmonica shall I start to play?" There are so
many types and styles of instruments -- single
and double hole Harmonicas --- instruments
with levers, buttons, bells and gadgets- big
Harmonicas and little Harmonicas. You have
heard them called "diatonic", "tremolo",
"concert" and "chromatic". There are also
many different keys --- "C", "D", "E", "F",
"G", "A" and "B". This might sound a bit
complicated and confusing, but it won't be for
long.

The Simple Ten-Hole Harmonica

You, as a new Harmonica student, will soon
understand what the experienced player already
knows, that a good, though inexpensive, Harmonica will suffice while you are learning to
play. For most practical purposes the best
one with which to start is the simple, 10-hole,
diatonic Harmonica, that is, the one without
sharps or flats. This is generally about four

inches in length and has ten holes, or air chambers, containing twenty reeds or notes. This type of instrument will fully answer your needs as a beginner and will enable you to get started with the least effort and expense.

There are now available, at most musical instrument supply dealers, a number of newly designed and improved Harmonicas. With a Harmonica tuned in the Key of "C" (the simplest and most popular key for the beginner) you are ready to start your musical career.

Points to Remember

1. To keep reeds from becoming too strained, do NOT play your Harmonica too loudly.

2. Take care of your Harmonica and your Harmonica will "take care of you".

3. When not in use, always keep your Harmonica in a dry, warm place.

4. Keep your Harmonica covered at all times, when you are not playing it, even when you put it in your pocket.

5. Do NOT try to make major repairs on your Harmonica unless you know EXACTLY what to do.

6. Your Harmonica needs "rest" - and if you give it "rest" it will last much longer.

7. When you play, try to keep your mouth dry and your Harmonica clean.

8. Dry your lips between each exercise and song you play so that moisture will not get into your Harmonica.

9. Keeping your Harmonica dry keeps it in better condition.

10. For the most practical purposes the best Harmonica with which to start, is the simple 10-hole, diatonic, tuned in the Key of C.

LESSON TWO

Basic Elements of the Simple "Numbers System"

The elementary system of playing Harmonica music designates the various notes in simple terms of BLOW and DRAW - followed by numbers from one to ten.

The reason is evident. Most of the present day Harmonicas have the air chambers, or holes, numbered. When the Harmonica is held in your left hand, ready to play, the low numbers which are the low notes should be on the left.

In the simple 10-hole, diatonic Harmonica, such as we now are discussing, you will find a range of almost three octaves. However, three notes are missing, "F" and "A" in the first octave, and "B" in the third octave. For practical purposes these three notes are omitted, so as not to disrupt the formation of the chords; more about this later.

Holding the Harmonica

As with any other musical instrument you should first learn the proper method of holding the Harmonica. Bearing in mind that the low notes should be to the left, grasp your Harmonica firmly between the index finger and the thumb on your left hand as shown below.

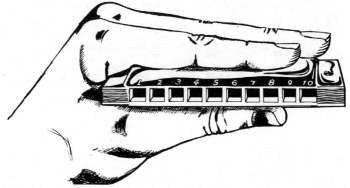

At this time you need not be concerned with your right hand. Later on we will discuss the importance of its proper use relative to achieving correct playing technique. To get "the feel" of playing, you should **BLOW** and DRAW gently, at random, going from low notes to high notes and back again. This will accustom you to the sound of the Harmonica tones.

The Notes and Holes of the Scale and How to Play Them

Diatonic Scale Begins at Hole No. 4

For the present concentrate your attention on the actual scale, which starts at HOLE #4 and then continues upward. A full diatonic scale (the scale without sharps - ♯ - or flats - ♭-) is contained in the holes Nos. 4, 5, 6, and 7. To familiarize yourself with the simple diatonic scale just pucker your lips as though you were going to whistle, then place them to Hole No.

4 and blow gently. The note that responds will be the first note of the scale and is called "Do." The following illustration shows where the lips should be placed for each note of the scale.

Now, keeping the lips in the same position, DRAW (breathe in) on Hole No. 4. The responding note will sound the second note in the scale, or "Re".

Maintaining the same position of the lips, move your Harmonica slightly to the left, in order to bring Hole No. 5 into position. BLOW Hole No. 5 and the note produced will be the third

note in the scale, or "Mi"; DRAW Hole No. 5 and the note produced will be the fourth note in the scale or "Fa". Move your Harmonica slightly to the left again and BLOW Hole No. 6.

This produces the sound of the fifth note in the scale, or "Sol". DRAW Hole No. 6 and you will get the sound of the sixth note in the scale "La". Move your Harmonica slightly to the left again and PAUSE.

The One Important Change in the Regularity of the Scale

At this point you should note very carefully that there is a change in the BLOW and DRAW arrangement. For Hole No. 7 the note is DRAWN first. In other words, DRAW 7 prod-

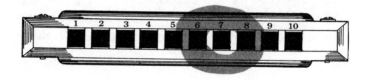

uces the 7th. note in the scale or, "Ti" and BLOW Hole No. 7 produces the 8th. note of the complete Diatonic Scale or, "Do". The exercise that follows below shows the complete Diatonic Scale, as just executed.

EXERCISE

Blow Draw Blow Draw Blow Draw Draw Blow
  4   4   5   5   6   6   7   7
"do" "re" "mi" "fa" "sol" "la" "ti" "do"

This first playing of the scale will sound somewhat uneven in tone, but by following the above exercise and practicing it for a minute or two, you will find that it is really quite simple. Be sure to REMEMBER that when you come to Hole No. 7, to first DRAW and then BLOW. The scale should be played over and over again following the Exercise = BLOWING and DRAW-ING until all the notes in the simple, diatonic scale are thoroughly familiar to you.

Now play the continuing notes; which are:
(See Illustrations below)

DRAW	BLOW	DRAW	BLOW	DRAW	BLOW
8	8	9	9	10	10
"Re"	"Mi"	"Fa"	"Sol"	"La"	"Do"

"Ti" is omitted in the third octave on the sim-ple, 10-hole Harmonica. You should now know where all the notes of the scale are located.

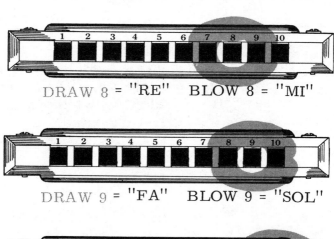

DRAW 8 = "RE"   BLOW 8 = "MI"

DRAW 9 = "FA"   BLOW 9 = "SOL"

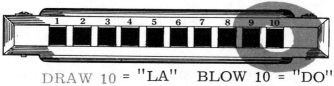

DRAW 10 = "LA"   BLOW 10 = "DO"

Summary of Lesson Two

Points to Remember

1. Hold your Harmonica in your LEFT hand, low notes or numbers to the left.

2. Do not be concerned with the use of your right hand. You will learn about this in later lessons.

3. Study the illustrations carefully while comparing your Harmonica with them. This will make playing much easier to master.

4. Remember the change in rotation starting with Hole No. 7. First DRAW and then BLOW to end the simple, diatonic scale.

5. Keep playing the scales until your "sound" is smooth.

6. PRACTICE makes perfect!

LESSON THREE

Single Tones

In the first lesson, when you played the simple scale, you no doubt encountered the same difficulty which most beginners do = TWO or THREE notes responded when you intended to play only ONE. For instance, when you attempted to BLOW No. 5, or "Mi", your lips were placed on Hole No. 5 but, as you sounded the note, air escaped from the corners of your mouth and was distributed over Holes Nos. 4, 5, and 6. However, as most of the breath was concentrated on the 5th hole, this note sounded the most predominant. You could not have avoided a little air creeping into the holes, on either side of No. 5, causing these reeds to respond also.

Obtaining the Single Note

All beginners find it difficult to learn to play the single note, so don't let it bother or discourage you. It is a difficulty very easy to overcome as you will learn in the following instructions. To obtain the sound of the single note, return to the scale which starts at Hole No. 4 and continues through Hole No. 7.

Until you learn the proper method of "TON-GUE - ING", which means the correct way of placing the TONGUE on the Harmonica, in order to obtain the single tone and also the bass accompaniment, hold your Harmonica in your left hand. Now place the index finger of your left hand on Hole Nos. 1, 2 and 3. At the same time place the index finger of your right hand on Hole Nos. 5, 6, 7 and 8, as shown in the following illustrations.

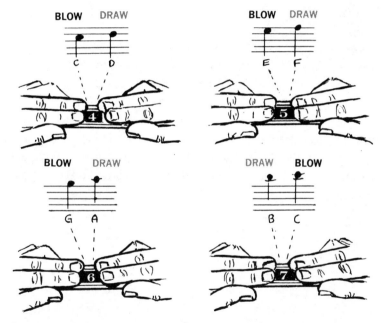

This will expose only Hole No. 4. Before sounding this note, be sure to see that Hole No. 3 is well covered with the index finger of your left hand.

Hold the instrument securely in that position. Press your lips over your finger tips and Hole

No. 4 and **BLOW**. The result should be a sharp and distinct tone. Now DRAW the same hole for the next note. Either way there should be a sound of ONE clear, distinct note.

The Importance of the Single Tone

The importance of the single tone will increase in significance as you progress. You will find that upon the quality of this single tone will depend much of your future excellence in your Harmonica technique.

Play the fore-going exercises; go up and down the scale keeping the index fingers alongside of each note while it is being played.

When you have mastered this, you will be ready for the "Professional Method" of playing known as "TONGUE-ING". The index finger method is used here solely to illustrate what is meant by the Single Tone.

Points to Remember

1. Try for clean, sharp, SINGLE notes.

2. The SINGLE Tone is necessary for effective, professional technique.

3. Aim for QUALITY of tone - Not Volume.

4. YOU are the master of how well you will play. It all depends on how much time you wish to devote to developing your technique.

LESSON FOUR

The Important Phase
of "Tongue-ing"

In your previous lesson you attempted to master the Single Note, by placing your index
fingers on either side of the note to be played
to prevent air from passing through more than
one hole, or air chamber, at a time. While
this method is effective in sounding the single
note, you cannot continue to play songs in this
manner. It will not be possible for you to
cover and uncover the necessary notes fast
enough.

It is necessary therefore, to replace this
method by using the proper "TONGUE-ING"
technique. The use of the finger on your left
hand should be replaced by the use of your
tongue and the use of your lips will replace
the use of your right index finger.

Normally the lips can cover about four holes
on the harmonica and, if you rest the tongue
against the instrument, it will cover three
holes, leaving one open to be played.

Proper "Tongue-ing"
to Obtain the Single Note
and for Playing the Scale

Starting at the left hand side of your Harmonica, with your lips covering the first four holes and your tongue resting on the first three, Hole No. 4 is exposed for playing. See following illustration.

Press your tongue firmly against the first three holes and BLOW gently through the corner of your mouth into Hole No. 4, to sound "Do". With your lips and your tongue in the same position DRAW 4 and sound "Re". The diagrams illustrate this principle and by following them, with a little practice, you will soon be able to play clean, single notes when you start to play the scale.

BLOW 5 = "ME"   DRAW 5 = "FA"

BLOW 6 = "SOL"   DRAW 6 = "LA"

DRAW 7 = "TI"   BLOW 7 = "DO"

At this point you may have some difficulty in trying to keep your tongue in the correct position to cover three holes while you BLOW or DRAW in the fourth hole. Don't get discouraged and DON'T HURRY through this lesson until you have completely mastered the principle of this important step.

The lesson that follows shows how to play the scale with the correct method of "TONGUEING".

UP:

Blow	Draw	Blow	Draw	Blow	Draw	Draw	Blow
4	4	5	5	6	6	7	7
"Do"	"Re"	"Mi"	"Fa"	"Sol"	"La"	"Ti"	"Do"

DOWN:

Blow	Draw	Draw	Blow	Draw	Blow	Draw	Blow
7	7	6	6	5	5	4	4
"Do"	"Ti"	"La"	"Sol"	"Fa"	"Mi"	"Re"	"Do"

When you can do this quickly and easily, you will have learned the simple, diatonic scale; the position of the scale on the Harmonica; the continuation of the scale; and how to obtain clean, single notes by using the lips and tongue.

To refresh your memory, here is the scale as found on your regular Harmonica tuned in the key of "C".

31

Blow	Draw	Blow	Draw	Blow	Draw	Draw	Blow
4	4	5	5	6	6	7	7
"Do"	"Re"	"Mi"	"Fa"	"Sol"	"La"	"Ti"	"Do"

DRAW	BLOW	DRAW	BLOW	DRAW	BLOW
8	8	9	9	10	10
"Re"	"Mi"	"Fa"	"Sol"	"La"	"Do"

Points to Remember

1. For proper "TONGUE-ING" the lips should cover four holes and the tongue should cover three holes.

2. If more than one note responds, your tongue is not properly placed on the Harmonica.

3. Practice your "TONGUE-ING" so that you will have no difficulty in placing your tongue and your lips and so that you will immediately strike the note you wish to play.

4. Practice this lesson until you can follow instructions for proper "TONGUE-ING" without having to "think" about what you are doing.

5. When you have perfected point 4, you will be "on your way" to a more professional approach.

6. Without playing it, MEMORIZE the scale by name and number.

7. When you have perfected point 6 then PLAY the scale.

LESSON FIVE

The Harmonica Playing Student

So far in your instruction the subject of time and rhythm has not been covered. It is the expressed purpose of this course "to teach" the "student" how to play at once and as quickly as possible because, "playing students" will learn the technical terms of musical scores more readily as they proceed. By including familiar songs in early lessons you will automatically sense the phrasing and rhythm of the song you are learning to play.

As you advance and familiarize yourself with the location of the various notes or "holes" of the Harmonica, the words of the song will be omitted and you will be taught to read time, rhythm and phrasing, all by the "Numbers System".

If you have been diligently practicing Lessons No. 1, 2, and 3, you should now be familiar with the scale and be able to play it quickly and easily.

You are no doubt anxious to "try your skill" at playing "a real song". Well, here it is; the tune is an old, familiar favorite, the words and numbers are plainly written. See page 71.

Practice this song two or three times, slowly at first, to get the knack of it, then with as much "shading" expression and feeling as possible.

Observe carefully the numbered notes. Hum the song to yourself - (NOT INTO THE HARMONICA) - to maintain the rhythm.

After a little practice, the song will come quite easily to you. Try to play with clear, single tones.

Points to Remember

1. Review where each numbered hole is on the Harmonica.

2. Be sure you are thoroughly familiar with the simple scale.

3. Hum the melody of the song to yourself, NOT INTO THE HARMONICA.

4. Play the song SLOWLY and, as you learn it, GRADUALLY increase the tempo.

5. "TONGUE-ING" your Harmonica properly is important. KEEP PRACTICING!

OLD FOLKS AT HOME

WAY DOWN UP-ON THE SWAN-EE RIV-ER

FAR, FAR A—WAY, THER'S WHERE MY HEART IS

TURN-ING EV-ER —THERE'S WHERE THE OLD FOLKS STAY.

ALL THE WORLD IS SAD AND WEA-RY EV'RY-WHERE I

ROAM, O HOW MY LONE-LY HEART GROWS WEARY—

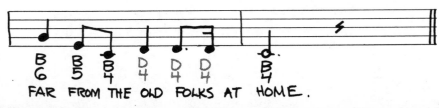

FAR FROM THE OLD FOLKS AT HOME.

LESSON SIX

How to Hold Your Harmonica
to Obtain "Vibrato"
and Expression in Your Playing

Every artist injects, consciously or unconsciously, some of his personality into his playing. He has his own mannerisms or expressions regardless of what instrument he plays. He tries to get a distinctive expression into his playing. In Harmonica playing there are certain basic effects which are essential to the development of acquiring "The Professional Technique". Among these "effects", one of the easiest and most helpful to learn, is the one called "Vibrato" or "Tremolo".

Anyone who listens to music has no doubt, heard the "wavering" or "fluttering" tone a violinist produces by rapidly "shaking" his finger on the strings of his instrument. This undulating effect lends color and embellishes the tone. Before you can obtain the "vibrato" or "tremolo" effect, you must learn to hold the Harmonica and your hands in the proper position. You have seen the Harmonica held by players in a dozen different ways. However, there is only ONE correct way to hold your Harmonica; that correct way will not only conserve your energy but it will also be readily adaptable to the production of numerous "tricks" and "effects". See illustration below.

Grasp your Harmonica firmly between the index finger and the thumb of your left hand, the low notes should be to the left.

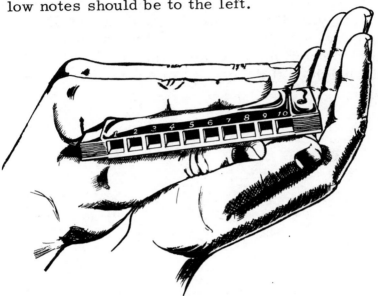

"Cupping" your Hands
for "Special Effects"

Place your Harmonica to your lips but not too deeply into your mouth. Now, bring the lower part of the PALM of your right hand close to the lower part of the PALM of your left hand, as shown above.

Pretend that your palms are "hinged" together and that they can be opened and closed like the cover of a book. This "CUPPING" of the hands forms an air or tone chamber, the opening and closing of which produces a delightful, "wavy" variation of tone. The speed with which you open and close your palms produces the various "Vibrato" effects. When you "stress" certain notes more than others you will find that you "catch on" very quickly to the principle involved and that you will be able to produce the effects you desire almost at once. A little practice with the songs you already know will quickly show you how much the "trick effects" will heighten the tone and improve your playing.

Points to Remember

1.   Practice, holding your Harmonica the correct way, in front of a mirror.

2.   Make a habit of playing with "Vibrato" - it sweetens the tone.

3.   Master the song in the previous lesson - LEARN IT "BY HEART".

4.   Play the song with "Vibrato" and note the difference in "the sound".

LESSON SEVEN

"TONGUE-ING"
with Bass Accompaniment

The proper use of the tongue cannot be stressed enough as an important factor in the correct playing of the Harmonica. It is especially important when, later on, you wish to produce such tonal values and effects as - "the trill; blue notes; slurs; train effects; organ tones; octave toning; bass accompaniment; rhythm beats; trumpet tones and many others." A full knowledge of these effects is essential for proper expression and interpretation.

Now we will consider one of the most important "TONGUE-ING" effects - that of "bass accompaniment". To do this, first blow a SINGLE note - (BLOW 4 will do), your lips should cover four notes and TONGUE should cover three notes. The sound should come out clear and sweet. Then to get the "bass accompaniment" simply lift your TONGUE away from your Harmonica, exposing hole Nos. 1 - 2 - 3 - 4. When you blow while your TONGUE is in this position a "chord" of four notes - "C" "E" "G" and "C" is produced.

Do not move your Harmonica nor change the position of your mouth - unless the music calls for a change from one note to another. The "chord" you have just produced was caused by the air passing through the four holes exposed when your TONGUE was raised. After blowing the "chord" play the single note again by bringing your TONGUE back to your Harmonica in its original position. (TONGUE covering three holes - lips covering four holes.)

You should now be playing - Single note - "chord" - then a single note. Try this a few times, SLOWLY at first, then FASTER, maintaining a regular beat or rhythm. This "bass accompaniment" can be played on the DRAW notes as well as on the BLOW notes. As indicated below, let's give it a try.

Scale with Bass Accompaniment

BLOW	BLOW	DRAW	DRAW	BLOW	BLOW
4	1-2-3-4	4	1-2-3-4	5	2-3-4-5

DRAW	DRAW	BLOW	BLOW	DRAW	DRAW
5	2-3-4-5	6	3-4-5-6	6	3-4-5-6

DRAW	DRAW	BLOW	BLOW
7	4-5-6-7	7	4-5-6-7

At this point you should be able to easily play the scale by single notes. Now let's try to play the scale using the "bass accompaniment" method. You are now actually doing two things at one time. You are playing the scale and keeping rapid time by tapping out the "bass accompaniment" with your TONGUE.

When you can rapidly play through the scale

with the "bass accompaniment" you will have mastered one of the most important techniques in the playing of the Harmonica. Then you will be ready for the next lesson.

Points to Remember

1. The importance of the proper use of the TONGUE cannot be stressed enough in the tonal effects you will get on your Harmonica.

2. When you MASTER this technique you will become, an "out-standing" Harmonica player, instead of an "ordinary" one.

3. Don't "by-pass" any of the instructions, this will HINDER rather than HELP you play well.

LESSON EIGHT

The Importance of "Bass Accompaniment"

As you know, whatever study you undertake, you reach a "test period". At this point you will be able to determine whether or not you wish to take seriously, your study of Harmonica playing. Also at this point, you should be able to solve "the puzzle" of "TONGUE-ING" and "BASS ACCOMPANIMENT". When you have done this you will find smooth sailing in your playing from then on.

Your effectiveness as a Harmonica player is entirely up to you. It is based on your mastery of the information presented in the previous and subsequent lessons.

The Importance of Time Value

The "secret" of time value, phrasing and correct rhythm depends on the proper use of your TONGUE. With your knowledge of "Bass Accompaniment" you will now learn just how it can be used in a few of its rhythmic forms.

Time value is the measure of time allotted to each note. The Harmonica is a genuine musical instrument. All musical terms and rules apply just as rigidly to it's proper playing as they do to the playing of any other. Consequently you can obtain on the Harmonica the same interpretation and phrasing of any song as you would on any other instrument.

The Use of Bass Accompaniment

The method of using the "Bass Accompaniment" can best be explained by the following:

It is natural, for anyone playing a song on any musical instrument, to keep time by tapping his foot in rhythm with the music. If the song is a Waltz the tap of the foot will be at 3 count intervals in the "phrasing" of the song - that is - one - two - three, one - two - three, etc. If the song is a slow Fox-trot, the tap of the foot will be at 4 count intervals - or - one - two - three - four, one - two - three - four, etc. If the songs are Jigs or Marches the tap of the foot would be at faster intervals.

In the use of "Bass Accompaniment" on your Harmonica, instead of keeping time with your foot you will be using your TONGUE in "tapping out" the rhythm. Let's "translate" foot tapping into the use of your TONGUE, like this:

Your TONGUE should be lifted from your Harmonica to "sound" the chord which is obtained by BLOWING and and DRAWING through any 4 holes on your Harmonica. Your TONGUE should immediately return to its natural position. This is the position used for obtaining the sound of the single note. (mouth covering four holes and TONGUE covering three.) Using this procedure keep in time with the song you are playing.

If it is a Waltz, you play three "Bass Accompaniment" chords to the measure, as you would if you were using your foot; that is - one - two - three, etc. The same rule applies to any song you play, the tempo of course, will be executed faster if the song is a march or jig, etc.

When you can play the "Bass Accompaniment" without "thinking" you will be ready to progress further. Each lesson is designed to "build" toward a more professional manner in your playing. Don't rush, patience will "pay off!"

Points to Remember

1. "Bass Accompaniment" is very important to Harmonica playing. The more you PRACTICE it the better you will play and the more PROFESSIONAL you will sound.

2. Remember the "steps" - Single Note - Chord - Single Note. These are the basics of "Bass Accompaniment".

3. "Bass Accompaniment" helps you to keep strict time and is very effective and important to the things you will learn next.

4. Just a reminder - Are you practicing your "Vibrato"?

LESSON NINE

The Importance of Tonal Quality

In rating the performance of any professional or amateur Harmonica player, judges attach great importance to tonal quality. You should therefore, give prime consideration to this. No matter how simple the tune, nor how technical, your tonal quality will determine whether or not you wish to become a serious or a non-serious Harmonica player. Just as a violinist is judged by the sweetness of his tones as well as his technical perfection, so is the Harmonica player evaluated.

Few people realize that the sound obtained on the Harmonica can be the sweetest, the fullest, the jazziest or the "thinnest" - all with the proper tonal quality.

Breathing Technique
For Good Tonal Quality

Proper breath control is the "secret" of the tone you produce. If you find yourself short of breath while playing, it indicates you will have to concentrate on perfecting your breathing technique. There is no mystery to this as you will learn in the instructions that follow. Don't RUSH, that makes you TENSE and you will NOT achieve the proper "breath technique" - when you relax, (take it easy) your "breath control" will improve.

Try this simple exercise:

> Starting with BLOW 7, take a deep breath and sound the note, sustaining it as long as your breath holds out. First play it LOUD and STRONG (without STRAINING the reeds of your Harmonica), then SOFTLY, allowing the BREATH to control the volume of sound. Then play BLOW 8 using the same procedure. Follow this with BLOW 9 and BLOW 10.

The strong, loud tones, you will observe are produced when all of the breath is concentrated directly on the reed chamber. No air should be permitted to escape through the corners of the mouth, through the nose, nor around nor over the Harmonica.

Now try the DRAW notes. Sustain them as long as possible. For the softer tones, allow half of the air to pass through the Harmonica and half of the air to pass through your nostrils. In this manner you will develop complete control of the volume of the sound you desire to produce. You can try the following exercises without using the VIBRATO or TREMOLO effects.

Play each note, allowing four slow beats to each note. Follow the instructions written BELOW each note. Sustain your breath until you have played all four notes.

Exercise

BLOW	BLOW	BLOW	BLOW
5	6	7	7
(softly)	(stronger)	(loud)	(softer)

BREATHE

BLOW	DRAW	BLOW	BLOW
7	8	9	8
(softly)	(softer)	(stronger)	(loud)

BREATHE

DRAW	BLOW	BLOW	DRAW
8	7	6	5
(louder)	(softer)	(softly)	(stronger)

BREATHE

BLOW	DRAW	DRAW	BLOW
5	6	5	4
(loud)	(softer)	(softly)	(softly)

Exercise for Breath Technique

Starting with BLOW 4, sound this note three times, clearly and distinctly in FAST time, without sustaining any beat - one - two - three; - one - two - three.

Now play the following short exercise in the way just indicated - three sharp notes QUICK-LY and DISTINCTLY ...

BREATHE

48

In the same way DRAW the following notes:

DRAW DRAW DRAW -- DRAW DRAW DRAW--
  4   4   4 -- 5   5   5 --

DRAW DRAW DRAW -- DRAW DRAW DRAW--
  6   6   6 -- 7   7   7 --

DRAW DRAW DRAW -- DRAW DRAW DRAW--
  6   6   6 -- 5   5   5 --

DRAW DRAW DRAW   Repeat the
  4   4   4   Above Exercise

Continued practice, only a few minutes every day, will make a marked difference in your playing.

Points to Remember

1. Breath control exercises will develop your breathing capacity and will also develop your chest and your shoulders.

2. Do NOT go on to the next lesson, until you can do EVERYTHING in this one, without becoming short of breath.

3. After a little practice, the exercises will become easier for you.

4. A Harmonica player is judged by his tone and breath control.

5. It isn't how LOUDLY you can play, but how WELL you can CONTROL the sweetness and mellowness of your tones.

6. Are you practicing your "BASS ACCOMPANIMENT"?

PREFACE TO SONG SECTION

As you know you are learning to play the Harmonica by NUMBERS and BLOW and DRAW indications. It has been proven however that by the time you have completed all the lessons in this book you will have subconsciously learned to read music. This is why in addition to the NUMBERS and BLOW and DRAW, musical notes are also shown on each song which follows. This is also the reason for this method being so out - standingly effective. Everyone who has learned to play the Harmonica, "The Hal Leighton Way", has automatically learned to read music at the same time.

Notes

LESSON TEN

Basic Elements of Music

The following charts will acquaint you with the fundamentals of written music. They are included to show you the relationship between the numbers and the actual, musical notations.

There are different types of notes used in all music. These are shown on the next page. These notes are positioned on five horizontal lines called the STAFF.

This Is Called The STAFF

At the beginning of each STAFF is the musical symbol called the CLEFF. The STAFF is divided into units of time called MEASURES or BARS.

This Is Called   This Is Called A
The CLEFF   Measure Or BAR

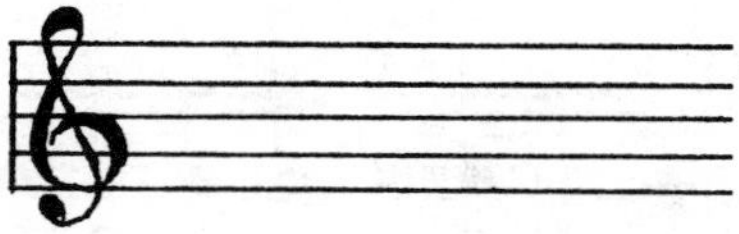

Different Type Notes

WHOLE — HALF — QUARTER — 8TH — 16TH

THE NOTES AND THEIR TIME VALUE

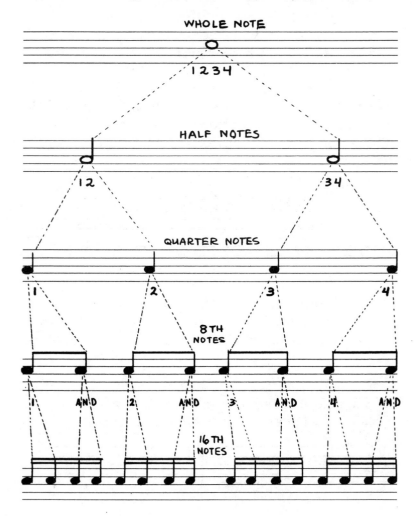

WHOLE NOTE

1 2 3 4

HALF NOTES

1 2   3 4

QUARTER NOTES

1   2   3   4

8TH NOTES

1 AND   2 AND   3 AND   4 AND

16TH NOTES

Names Of NOTES On The LINES

E G B D F

Names Of NOTES In The SPACES Between The Lines

F A C E

Each of the notes is given a different time value or beat. For example: A WHOLE note is given "4 beats" to each measure. A HALF note is given "2 beats" to each measure, etc.

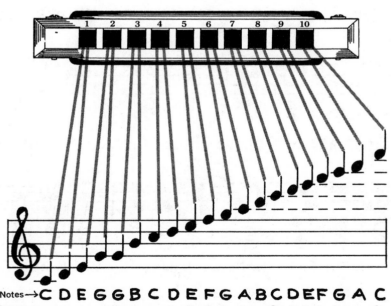

COMPLETE SCALE FOR 10 HOLE HARMONICA

Notes → C D E G G B C D E F G A B C D E F G A C

Blow or Draw for each Hole → B₁ D₁ B₂ D₂ B₃ D₃ B₄ D₄ B₅ D₅ B₆ D₆ D₇ B₇ D₈ B₈ D₉ B₉ D₁₀ B₁₀

HOME ON THE RANGE

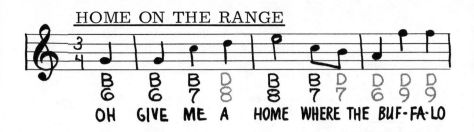

OH GIVE ME A HOME WHERE THE BUF-FA-LO

ROAM, WHERE THE DEER AND THE AN-TE-LOPE PLAY, WHERE

NEV-ER IS HEARD A DIS-COUR-AG-ING WORD, AND THE

SKIES ARE NOT CLOUD-Y ALL DAY.   HOME,

HOME ON THE RANGE, WHERE THE DEER AND THE

AN-TE-LOPE PLAY,   WHERE NEV-ER IS

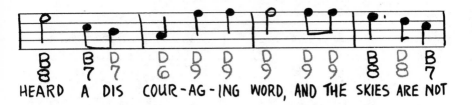

HEARD A DIS COUR-AG-ING WORD, AND THE SKIES ARE NOT

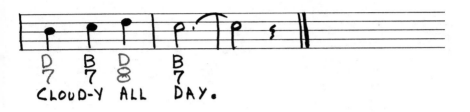

CLOUD-Y ALL DAY.

ROW, ROW, ROW YOUR BOAT

ROW, ROW, ROW, YOUR BOAT GENT-LY DOWN THE

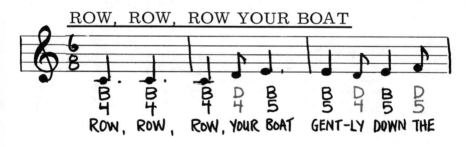

STREAM; MER-RI-LY, MER-RI-LY, MERRILY, MERRILY,

LIFE IS BUT A DREAM.

CLEMENTINE

IN A CAV-ERN IN A CAN-YON, EX-CA-

VAT-ING FOR A MINE, DWELT A MINER FOR-TY-

NIN-ER AND HIS DAUGHT-ER CLEM-EN-TINE. OH MY

DAR-LING, OH MY DAR-LING, OH MY DAR-LING CLEM-EN-

TINE, YOU ARE LOST AND GONE FOR-EV-ER! DREF-FUL

SOR-RY, CLEM-EN-TINE!

AMERICA, THE BEAUTIFUL

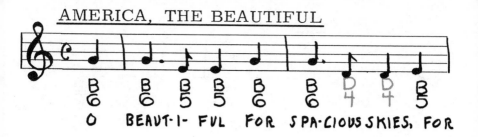

O BEAUT-I- FUL FOR SPA-CIOUS SKIES, FOR

AM-BER WAVES OF GRAIN. FOR PUR-PLE MOUN-TAIN

MAJ-ES-TIES A- BOVE THE FRUIT-ED PLAIN. A-

MER- I- CA, A- MER- I- CA, GOD SHED HIS GRACE ON

THEE. AND CROWN THY GOOD WITH BRO-THER-HOOD FROM

SEA TO SHIN- ING SEA.

MY BONNIE

MY BON-NIE LIES OV-ER THE O-CEAN,

MY BON-NIE LIES OV-ER THE SEA. MY

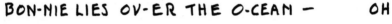

BON-NIE LIES OV-ER THE O-CEAN — OH

BRING BACK MY BON-NIE TO ME. BRING

BACK, BRING BACK, BRING BACK MY BON-NIE TO

ME, TO ME. BRING BACK, BRING BACK, OH

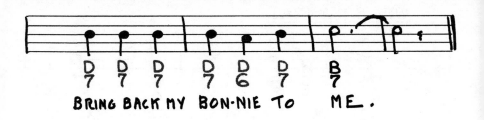

D D D D D D B
7 7 7 7 6 7 7

BRING BACK MY BON-NIE TO ME.

GOODNIGHT LADIES

B B B B B B D D
8 7 6 7 8 7 8 8

GOOD-NIGHT LA-DIES, GOOD-NIGHT LA-DIES,

B B D D D B B D D B
8 7 9 9 9 8 7 8 7 7

GOOD-NIGHT LA-DIES, WE'RE GOING TO LEAVE YOU NOW.

B D B D B B B D D D B B B
8 8 7 8 8 8 8 8 8 8 8 9 9

MER-RI-LY WE ROLL A-LONG ROLL A-LONG ROLL A-LONG

B D B D B B B D D B D B
8 8 7 8 8 8 8 8 8 8 8 7

MER-RI-LY WE ROLL A-LONG O'ER THE DEEP BLUE SEA.

OH, SUSANNA!

B4 D4 B5 B6 B6 D6 B6 B5 B4 D4
I WENT DOWN SOUTH TO SEE MY SAL-THE

B5 B5 D4 B4 D4 B4 D4 B5 B6 B6 D6
WEATH-ER IT WAS FINE. THE SUN SO HOT I

B6 B5 B4 D4 B5 B5 D4 D4 B4
FROZE TO DEATH- SU-SAN-NA, DON'T YOU PINE!

D5 D5 D6 D6 D6 B6 B6 B5 B4 D4 B4 D4
OH SU - SAN-NA, OH DON'T YOU PINE FOR ME- I'VE

B5 B6 B6 D6 B6 B5 B4 D4 B5 B5 D4 D4
COME FROM AL-A BAM-A WITH MY BAN-JO ON MY

B4
KNEE.

THREE BLIND MICE

THREE BLIND MICE, THREE BLIND MICE,

SEE HOW THEY RUN! SEE HOW THEY RUN! THEY

ALL RAN AF-TER THE FARMER'S WIFE SHE CUT OFF THEIR TAILS WITH A

CARV-ING KNIFE. DID YOU EV-ER SEE SUCH A

SIGHT IN YOUR LIFE AS THREE BLIND MICE!

YANKEE DOODLE

B B B D B   B B D B
7 7 7 8 8   7 8 8 6

FATH-ER AND I WENT DOWN TO CAMP A-

B B D B   B D B   B B D B
7 7 8 8   7 7 6   7 7 8 8

LONG WITH CAP-TAIN GOOD-WIN, AND THERE WE SAW THE

D B D B   D B D D   B B
9 8 8 7   7 6 6 7   7 7

MEN AND BOYS AS THICK AS HAS-TY PUD-DIN'.

D D D B   D D B   B D B D
6 7 6 6   6 7 7   6 6 6 5

YAN-KEE DOO-DLE, KEEP IT UP, YAN-KEE DOO-DLE

B B   D D D B   D D B D
5 6   6 7 6 6   6 7 7 6

DAN-DY, MIND THE MU-SIC AND THE STEP, AND

B B D D   B B
6 7 7 8   7 7

WITH THE GIRLS BE HAN-DY.

JINGLE BELLS

JIN-GLE BELLS, JIN-GLE BELLS, JIN-GLE ALL THE

WAY, OH WHAT FUN IT IS TO RIDE IN A

ONE-HOSS OP-EN SLEIGH! JIN-GLE BELLS,

JIN-GLE BELLS, JIN-GLE ALL THE WAY,

OH WHAT FUN IT IS TO RIDE IN A ONE-HOSS OP-EN

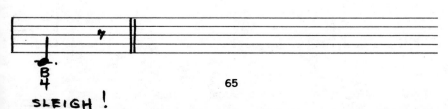

SLEIGH!

ON TOP OF OLD SMOKY

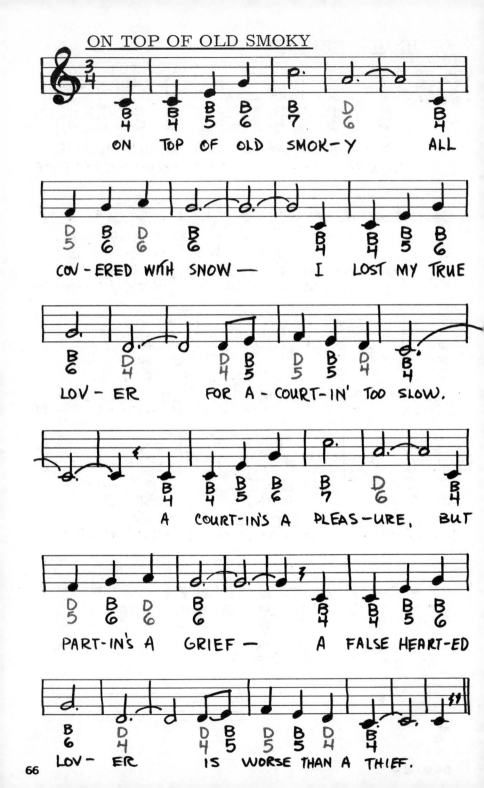

SHE'LL BE COMIN' 'ROUND THE MOUNTAIN

SHE'LL BE COM-IN' ROUND THE MOUN-TAIN WHEN SHE

COMES, SHE'LL BE COM-IN' ROUND THE MOUNT-AIN WHEN SHE

COMES. SHE'LL BE COMIN' ROUND THE MOUNT-AIN. SHE'LL BE

COM-IN' ROUND THE MOUNTAIN, SHE'LL BE COM-IN' ROUND THE

MOUNT-AIN WHEN SHE COMES.

DIXIE

I WISH I WAS IN THE LAND OF COT-TON-

OLD TIMES THERE ARE NOT FOR-GOTTEN- LOOK-A-WAY, LOOK A-

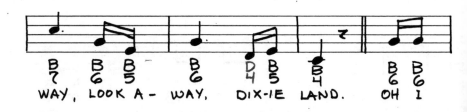

WAY, LOOK A- WAY, DIX-IE LAND. OH I

WISH I WAS IN DIX-IE, HOO-RAY, HOO-RAY! IN

DIX-IE-LAND I'LL TAKE MY STAND TO LIVE AND DIE IN

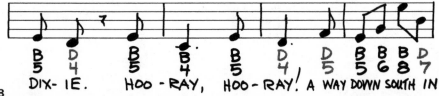

DIX-IE. HOO-RAY, HOO-RAY! A WAY DOWN SOUTH IN

D	B	B	B	B	D	D
8	7	5	4	5	4	6

DIX - IE.   A - WAY - A - WAY - A -

B	B	B	D	D	B
6	5	8	7	8	7

WAY DOWN SOUTH IN   DIX - IE !

BATTLE HYMN OF THE REPUBLIC

B	B	B	B	D	B	B	B	D
6	6	6	6	5	5	6	7	8

MINE   EYES HAVE SEEN THE GLO-RY OF THE

B	B	B	D	B	B	D	D	D	D	D
8	8	8	8	7	7	7	6	6	6	7

COM- ING OF THE LORD. HE IS TRAMP-ING OUT THE

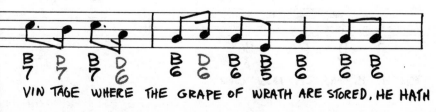

B	B	B	D	B	D	B	B	B	B	B
7	7	7	6	6	6	6	5	6	6	6

VIN TAGE WHERE THE GRAPE OF WRATH ARE STORED, HE HATH

B B B D B B B D
6 6 6 5 5 6 7 8

LOOSED THE FATE-FUL LIGHTNING OF HIS TER-R-BLE SWIFT

B B D D B D B
7 7 8 8 7 7 7

SWORD, HIS TRUTH IS MARCH-ING ON!

B D B B B D B B
6 5 5 6 7 8 8 7

GLO-RY GLO-RY HAL-LE-LU-JAH!

D D B D B D B B
6 7 7 7 7 6 6 5

GLOR-Y, GLORY HAL-LE-LU-JAH!

B D B B B D B B B
6 5 5 6 7 8 8 7 7

GLO-RY, GLO-RY HAL-LE-LU-JAH, HIS

D D B D B
8 8 7 7 7

TRUTH IS MARCH-ING ON!

HARMONICA SONG

WORDS AND MUSIC BY
FORMAN BROWN, ASCAP

B6 B6 B5 D5 B6 B7 B6 D5 B5 D5

I PLAY MY HAR-MON-I-CA ALL THE DAY

D4 D4 B5 D5 D4 B5 D5 D7 D6 B6 D6 B6

LONG. IF YOU KNOW HOW TO BREATHE YOU CAN NEV-ER GO

B5 B6 B6 B6 B5 D5 B6 B7 B6 D6 D5 D6

WRONG. IF YOU LEARN WHEN TO DRAW AND YOU LEARN WHEN TO

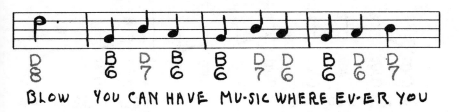

D8 B6 D7 B6 B6 D7 D6 B6 D6 D7

BLOW YOU CAN HAVE MU-SIC WHERE EV-ER YOU

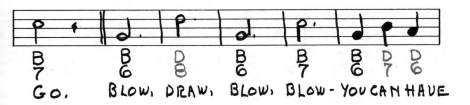

B7 B6 D8 B6 B7 B6 D7 D6

GO. BLOW, DRAW, BLOW, BLOW-YOU CAN HAVE

B6 D7 D6 B6 D6 D7 B7

MU-SIC WHERE EV-ER YOU GO.

71

MUSIC IN MY POCKET

WORDS AND MUSIC BY
FORMAN BROWN ASCAP

POCK-ET - THERE'S NO-THING QUITE SO SMART. FOR WITH

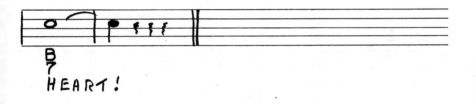

MU-SIC IN YOUR POCK-ET YOU'LL HAVE MU-SIC IN YOUR

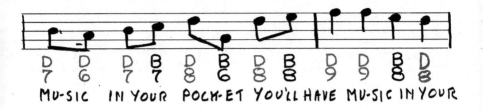

HEART!

THE SHINY HARMONICA

WORDS AND MUSIC BY FORMAN BROWN, ASCAP

WHEN I WAS A LAD THERE WAS ONE THING I

HAD—'TWAS THE JOY AND THE PRIDE OF MY LIFE.

I SAVED UP AND BOUGHT IT, AND I HAVE STILL

GOT IT, A- LONG WITH A CHILD AND A WIFE.

IT'S ON-LY A SHIN-Y HAR-MON-I-CA,

BUT I PLAY IT WHEN-EV-ER I'M BLUE.

B6 B8 B8 B8 B8 D8 B7

IF YOU NEED A FRIEND WHO IS

D6 D8 B8 D5 D9 B8 D8 B7

TRUE TO THE END, JUST BUY A HAR-

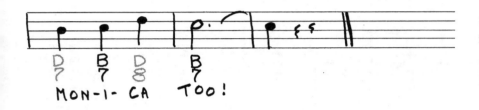

D7 B7 D8 B7

MON-I-CA TOO!

DRINK TO ME ONLY WITH THINE EYES

B5 B5 B5 D5 D5 B6 D5 B5 D4 B5 D5

DRINK TO ME ON-LY WITH THINE EYES, AND

B6 B4 D5 B5 D4 B4 B5 B5 B5

I WILL PLEDGE WITH MINE. OR LEAVE A

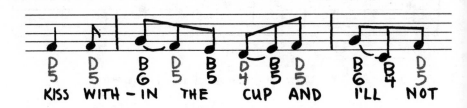

KISS WITH – IN THE CUP AND I'LL NOT

ASK FOR WINE. THE THIRST THAT FROM THE

SOUL DOTH RISE DOTH ASK A DRINK DI-

VINE. BUT MIGHT I OF JOVE'S NEC – TAR

SIP. I WOULD NOT CHANGE FOR THINE.

ANNIE LAURIE

MAX— WEL-TON'S BRAES ARE BON-NIE WHERE

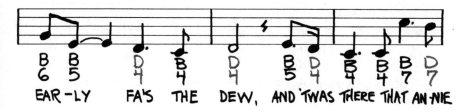

EAR-LY FA'S THE DEW, AND 'TWAS THERE THAT AN-NIE

LAU-RIE GAVE ME HER PROM-ISE TRUE. GAVE

ME HER PROM-ISE TRUE, WHICH NE'ER FOR-GOT WILL

BE, AND FOR BON-NIE AN-NIE LAU-RIE I'D

LAY ME DO'ON AND DEE.

BEAUTIFUL DREAMER

B7 D7 B7 B6 B5 D4 D4 D4 D6

BEAUT-I-FUL DREAM-ER WAKE UN-TO ME,

B6 D7 D6 D6 B6 D5 D5 B5 D4 B5

STAR-LIGHT AND DEW-DROPS ARE WAIT-ING FOR THEE.

B7 D7 B7 B6 B5 D4 D4 D4 D6

SOUNDS OF THE RUDE WORLD HEARD IN THE DAY

B6 D7 D6 D6 B6 D5 D5 B5 D4 B4

LULLED BY THE MOON-LIGHT HAVE ALL PASSED A-WAY.

B6 D5 D4 D3 D6 D6 B6 B5 B4

BEAUT-I-FUL DREAM-ER, QUEEN OF MY SONG,

B7 D7 B7 D6 D8 B7 D7 B7 B6 B6

LIST WHILE I WOO THEE WITH SWEET MEL-O-DY.

GONE ARE THE CARES OF LIFE'S BU-SY THRONG,

BEAUT-I-FUL DREAM-ER, A-WAKE UN-TO ME!

BEAUT-I-FUL DREAM-ER, A- WAKE UN-TO ME!

HAPPY BIRTHDAY

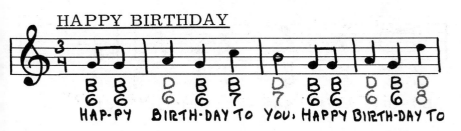

HAP-PY BIRTH-DAY TO YOU, HAPPY BIRTH-DAY TO

YOU! HAP-PY BIRTH-DAY, DEAR SAL-LY - HAP-PY

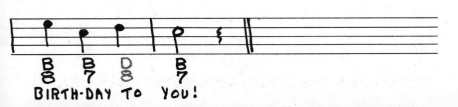

BIRTH-DAY TO YOU!

SANTA LUCIA

O MOON WHOSE MYSTIC VEIL, FROM THE SKIES

FALL-ING, GILDS SIGH-ING WAT-ERS PALE, TO OUR HEART

CALL-ING. GLOR-IOUS THE SUM-MER NIGHT, SEA-STRAND AND

BIL-LOWS WHITE — SAN — TA — LU — CI — A —

SAN — TA LU — CI — A!

HOME SWEET HOME

MID PLEAS-URES AND PAL-AC-ES

THOUGH WE MAY ROAM, BE IT EV - ER SO

HUM-BLE, THERE'S NO PLACE LIKE HOME.

HOME, HOME, SWEET, SWEET HOME! THERE'S NO PLACE LIKE

HOME, NO, THERE'S NO PLACE LIKE HOME.

You are now ready to attempt your first song with musical notes alone. The hole numbers have been removed on this song.

HOME SWEET HOME

MID   PLEAS-URES AND PAL-AC-ES

THOUGH WE MAY ROAM, BE IT EV- ER SO

HUM-BLE, THERE'S NO   PLACE LIKE HOME.

HOME , HOME,   SWEET ,SWEET HOME! THERE'S NO PLACE LIKE

HOME , NO, THERE'S NO PLACE LIKE HOME.

PART TWO

Trick Effects

Notes

LESSON ELEVEN

Some Simple "Trick" Effects

"TRILLING"

Before you can become really proficient in playing the Harmonica, you must MASTER many "trick effects". Some are complicated - others are very simple. Each of these "trick effects" is as important as the other and each one has its very definite place in the pattern of playing Harmonica music.

If you remember that the Harmonica, compared to other musical instruments, has certain limitations, you will understand the necessity for and the importance of these "trick effects". They will help to improve the quality of your music and of the technique you use and will make your playing more interesting and effective.

Mastering the "TRILL"

"Trilling" is very popular with both the amateur and the professional players and is not at all difficult to learn. It is produced by rapidly rolling the TONGUE against the roof of the mouth, just back of the upper teeth. The sound is that of "rolling" a long "R" or -- trr - trr - trr - trr. Place your lips on your Harmonica as though you are going to play a single note and try the "trill" effect.

"Trilling" is achieved most effectively by starting on the left side of your Harmonica and sweeping up to a sustained, "trilled" note. Chord "trills" are obtained by "trilling" three or four notes at the same time and by moving along the Harmonica. Drum effects; airplane effects and many others are all variations of "trilling".

The Chucka - Chucka Effect

In Lesson No. 7, you studied the "Bass Accompaniment". Using the "Bass Accompaniment" you will be able to master another useful Harmonica "secret". With this technique you will, in effect, be making the Harmonica "talk". This is called "Chugging"-or-"chucka - chucka". It is produced on the first four Holes or BLOW notes of the Harmonica. All you have to do is SPEAK into the Harmonica, pronouncing the words, "chucka - chucka". The Harmonica, you will find, SPEAKS the same thing. Do the same thing on the DRAW notes as well. This "chucka - chucka" effect is the basis for producing "train imitations" as well as supplying the background of rhythm accompaniment in orchestral work.

The Train Effect

Starting slowly, in regular rhythm, say - "chucka - chucka". Now, gradually increase the rhythm, but maintain a regular beat. Cup your hands over your Harmonica, this you will find will produce a change in tone. As you continue to speed up the rhythm, open and close your cupped hands. This will give you an effect that approximates the sound of a train in motion. Naturally, your own ear will tell you how well you are doing your imitation of a moving train.

To get the effect of a "train whistle", you must "trill" the high note, this will sound as though your "musical train" is about to reach a "Rail-Road Crossing". This effect is great fun once you master it.

Points to Remember

1. Trick effects enhance your playing and help you to master the playing of any "sound" you wish to produce on your Harmonica.

2. Most effects that can be produced on the Harmonica CANNOT be duplicated on any other instrument.

3. Trick effects are very important when played correctly in the proper part of a song.

4. How long can you "trill" a note? If you can't for very long, you need a little more PRACTICE in your lesson on "Breath Control".

LESSON TWELVE

The Music Box

Playing the high notes on the Harmonica will produce the effect of "Music Box" tones. The exercise which follows, when played fast and distinctly, using a clear, single tone will give a "Tinkling Music Box" sound.

Exercise

Blow Blow Blow Blow Blow Blow Blow Blow
  9   8   7   8   9   8   7   8

Draw Draw Draw Draw Draw Draw Draw Draw
  9   8   7   8   9   8   7   8

(Repeat Above Exercise)

The Hot Trumpet

Effects on the Harmonica to produce the sound of the "Hot Trumpet", "Hot Choruses" and syncopated "Jazz Rhythms" can be obtained as follows:

Cup your hands tightly around your Harmonica and sound TWO notes together - BLOW 4 and 5. The muffled tone simulates that which the trumpet player produces when he places a "derby" over the bell of his instrument. As he plays he waves the hat (derby) back and forth causing the tone to undulate. When you open and close your "cupped" hands while you are BLOWING notes 4 and 5, you are imitating the sound that the trumpet player makes by the movement of the "derby". The "split second" opening of your "cupped" hands causes a change in the tone which can be further embellished by "trilling" from the back of your throat. This adds a guttural quality to the notes.

Play in rhythm opening your "cupped" hands on the OFF - BEATS, or more specifically, "trill" from the back of your throat, similar to the method used when you "gargle".

"Drums"

"Drum Beats" can effectively be reproduced, by "trilling" simultaneously, into "THREE" out of "FOUR" holes, while "MOVING" up and down on your Harmonica to produce variations in pitch. You get this "drum sound" by actually pronouncing the words (into your Harmonica) BURRMMM - BURRMMM - BURRMMM - maintaining the same rhythm as a drummer would. On your Harmonica however, you will be "tapping out the drum beats" with your TONGUE

"Blue-ing"

"Blue notes" are produced on your Harmonica, when your lips are "formed" over a SINGLE hole as though you are going to whistle. Contract your LIPS and your TONGUE, while forcing your breath through the SINGLE hole and pronounce the word "yoe-ee". The resulting tone will be a half or a quarter tone LOWER than the original note. A well-controlled "blue note" is very effective in playing jazz rhythms. Constant practice is an absolute necessity. Once you master this technique you will find frequent use for it. The notes best suited for "Blue-ing" (on a ten hole Harmonica) are:

Draw 6, Blow 7, Blow 8, Blow 9, Blow 10.

"The Glass Tone"

This favorite effect, used by Harmonica Players, is produced by using a glass tumbler in the same way as the Trumpet Player uses the "derby". It gives the sound of a beautiful, organ-toned vibrato. The LOW notes, because of their deeper, more vibrant tones are especially effective.

"Moan-ing"

The "MOAN-ING" effect is produced on the LOW notes of the Harmonica. It is a combination of a blue note and a muffled tone. This is obtained by tightly "cupping" your hands around your Harmonica and playing a LOW note, as though you intended to "blue" it. BLOW easily but firmly, and as the note begins to respond open your "cupped" hands in rhythm to get a "MOAN-ING" effect, which would sound as though you were "saying"..."Wah - wah" - "wah - wah". The "MOAN-ING" tone is one of the most advanced "trick effects" used exclusively by Professional Harmonica Players.

Points to Remember

1. You should carefully study all the "Trick Effects" and know how to play them without having to refer to the lesson.

2. "Trick Effects" will become an important part of your technique in playing in a more professional manner.

3. In accompanying other players you will find the "Chugga - Chugga" effect excellent for Rhythm Accompaniment.

4. You are reminded to REVIEW all the previous lessons before advancing to the next lesson.

Notes

PART THREE

The 10 Hole

Chromatic Harmonica

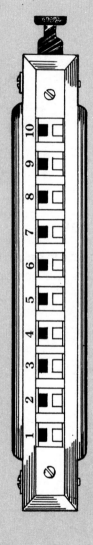

10 HOLE CHROMATIC HARMONICA

NATURAL SIZE

LESSON THIRTEEN

How to Play
The 10-Hole Chromatic Harmonica
and its Construction

(See Illustration on Page 94)

The most apparent physical difference is the lever or key-changing shutter enclosed in the metal mouth-piece. When the lever is in the "OUT" position, it exposes the upper row of notes which are arranged in a diatonic scale. When the lever is pressed "IN", it exposes the lower row of notes which contain the half-tones or sharps and flats and are equivalent to the black keys on the piano.

The 10-Hole Chromatic Harmonica has two and a half chromatic scales. To acquaint you with the 10-Hole Chromatic, first learn to play the simple diatonic scales. The first scale starts at BLOW 1 to BLOW 4 - the "basic" second scale starts at BLOW 5 to BLOW 8. The holes 9 and 10 comprise the half scale or unfinished third scale.

See Next Page for Diatonic Scale and Correct Tongue-ing.

TONGUE-ING THE 10-HOLE CHROMATIC

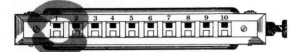

BLOW 1 = "C"   DRAW 1 = "D"

BLOW 2 = "E"   DRAW 2 = "F"

BLOW 3 = "G"   DRAW 3 = "A"

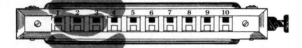

DRAW 4 = "B"   BLOW 4 = "C"

BLOW 5 = "C"   DRAW 5 = "D"

BLOW 6 = "E"   DRAW 6 = "F"

BLOW 7 = "G"   DRAW 7 = "A"

DRAW 8 = "B"   BLOW 8 = "C"

Hold your 10-Hole Chromatic Harmonica in the left hand with the low notes to your left. Grip your instrument between your index finger and thumb. This leaves your right hand free for obtaining vibrato effects and for manipulating the lever, as shown below.

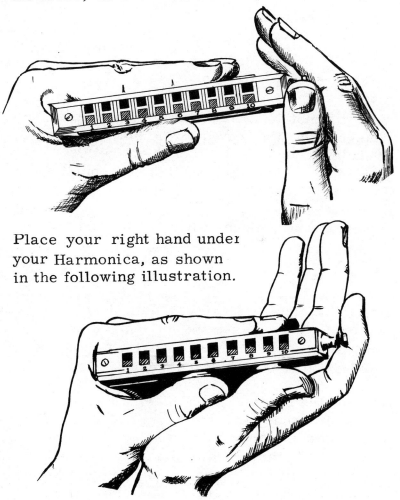

Place your right hand under your Harmonica, as shown in the following illustration.

The lever should be controlled by the index finger of your right hand. When "Cupped" your right hand forms an air chamber. This is the most practical way to hold your Harmonica and it will make it much easier for you to master the more advanced techniques and trick effects. Now play the simple, diatonic scale as follows; starting on "BLOW 5" and continuing up the scale.

Blow	Draw	Blow	Draw	Blow	Draw	Draw	Blow
5	5	6	6	7	7	8	8

You will notice that there is absolutely no change from the way that you play the simple, 10-hole Harmonica. By pushing the lever IN, you will find the tone is that of a completely "new" sounding Harmonica.

Observe what happens when you do this. When the lever is OUT, the top holes are open.

See illustration at Right ▷

Press the lever IN and it acts just like a shutter. You will see the top holes close and the bottom row of holes open. This then becomes your "second" Harmonica.

Holding the lever IN, try playing the scale in the same manner starting from BLOW 5. You will immediately notice that this produces "another" diatonic scale, but it is pitched or tuned, one-half tone higher than when you played the scale with the slide OUT.

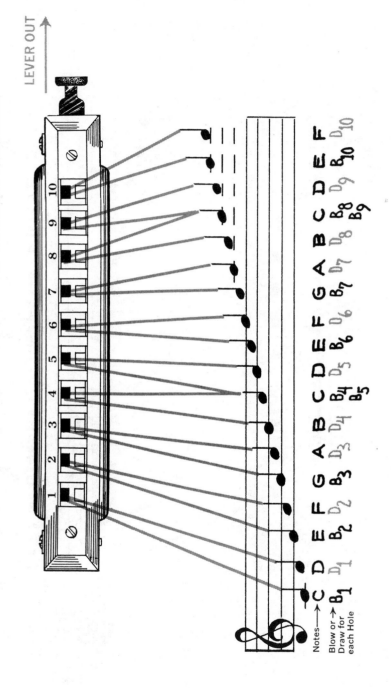

COMPLETE DIATONIC SCALE FOR 10 HOLE CHROMATIC HARMONICA WITH SHARPS

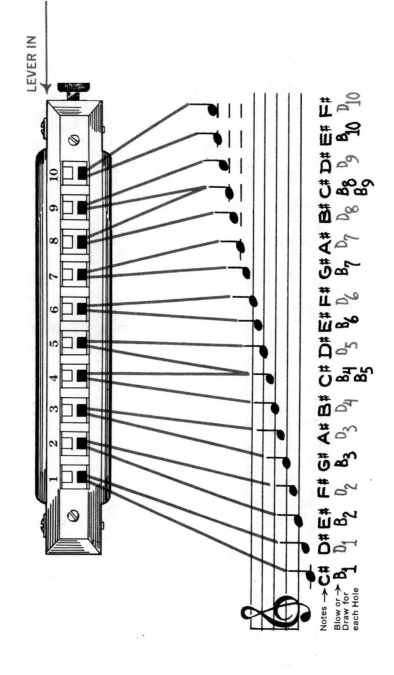

Construction

Observe how simply this Chromatic Harmonica is constructed. It comprises "two, simple" Harmonicas built into one. In other words, it has a simple scale when the lever is OUT and another simple scale, tuned one-half a tone higher, when the lever is pushed IN. See illustration on Page 100. The importance of these two simple scales combined, is that you get the necessary notes or tones you need to be able to play any piece of music in any key.

The next step is learning how to play these "two, combined" scales to make them sound like "One" which, in fact, they really are.

Play the following notes, keeping in mind that when a "sharp" sign (#) appears before the number, this means that you should play the note with the slide IN. When there is no "sharp" sign (#) before the number you should play the note with the slide OUT.

EXAMPLE: When you see BLOW 5, play BLOW 5, with the lever OUT. Don't concern yourself with the use of the lever until you see the "sharp" sign, (#). BLOW #5 means to play the same hole while pressing the lever IN, as far as it will go.

Now play the Chromatic Scale going up, using the same principle that you did in playing the scale on the "simple" Harmonica, as follows:

Blow Blow Draw Draw Blow Draw Draw Blow
  5   #5   5   #5   6   6   #6   7

      Blow Draw Draw Draw Blow
       #7   7   #7   8   8

Now play the Chromatic Scale, going down

Blow Draw Draw Draw Blow Blow Draw Draw
  8   8   #7   7   #7   7   #6   6

      Blow Draw Draw Blow Blow
       6   #5   5   #5   5

Points to Remember

1. When you use the lever, while playing, you sound your "second" Harmonica, which is tuned one half-tone higher.

2. Practice your Chromatic Scale until you can play it without thinking.

3. Learn the proper way to hold your Chromatic Harmonica.

4. Learn all that you can about your Chromatic Harmonica . It has all the possibilities for allowing you to play all types of music.

5. Don't go on to the next lesson until you have mastered this one.

SPRING SONG

MENDELSOHN

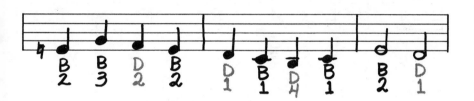

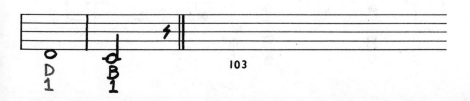

OVER THE WAVES

SWEET AND LOW

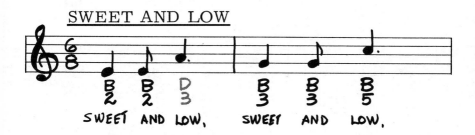

SWEET AND LOW, SWEET AND LOW,

WIND OF THE WEST-ERN SEA.

LOW, LOW, BREATHE AND BLOW, WIND OF THE WEST-ERN

PART FOUR

The 12 Hole
Chromatic Harmonica

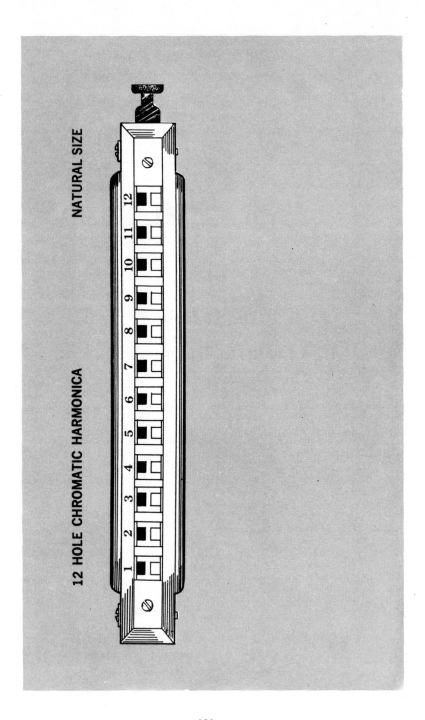

12 HOLE CHROMATIC HARMONICA

NATURAL SIZE

LESSON FOURTEEN

How to Play the 12-Hole Chromatic Harmonica

The 12-Hole, Chromatic Harmonica is recommended for you students who have MASTERED the playing of the 10-Hole Chromatic. It is "THE HARMONICA" which is played by all professional soloists. When you have mastered the 10-Hole Chromatic you will find that it will be just as easy to play the 12-Hole, Chromatic Harmonica. See illustration on Page 108.

Construction

With a few variations in principle, the 12-Hole Chromatic is the same as the 10-Hole Chromatic. The most apparent physical difference between the 10-Hole and the 12-Hole Chromatics is that the 12-Hole has a three octave, chromatic range. Since you do have this three octave range you will find that B/4 and B/5 also B/8 and B/9 will repeat. The reason for this is that the octave is complete within itself.

1st Octave } starts with B/1 and ends with B/4.

2nd Octave } starts with B/5 and ends with B/8.

3rd Octave } starts with B/9 and ends with B/12.

How to Hold the 12-Hole Chromatic Harmonica

You will hold your 12-Hole,Chromatic Harmonica in exactly the same way in which you held your 10-Hole Chromatic. For your convenience the instructions are repeated here. With the low notes to your left, hold your 12-Hole, Chromatic Harmonica in your left hand, firmly grip it between your index finger and your thumb.

This leaves your right hand free for obtaining vibrato effects and for manipulating the lever. Place your right hand under your Harmonica, (AS SHOWN IN THE ILLUSTRATION FOR THE 10-HOLE CHROMATIC ON PAGE 97. The lever should be controlled by the index finger of your right hand which, as you know, when "Cupped" will form an air chamber. This as already stated in Lesson 13, page 97 is the most practical way to hold your Harmonica for mastering the professional way of playing.

"Tongue-ing" for the 12-Hole Chromatic Harmonica

You can obtain the single tones on the 12-Hole Chromatic by using the same "Tongue-ing" as shown in the following illustration.

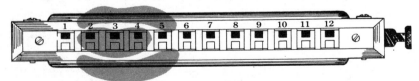

(Additional Tongue-ing diagrams on Page 96.)

COMPLETE DIATONIC SCALE FOR 12 HOLE CHROMATIC HARMONICA

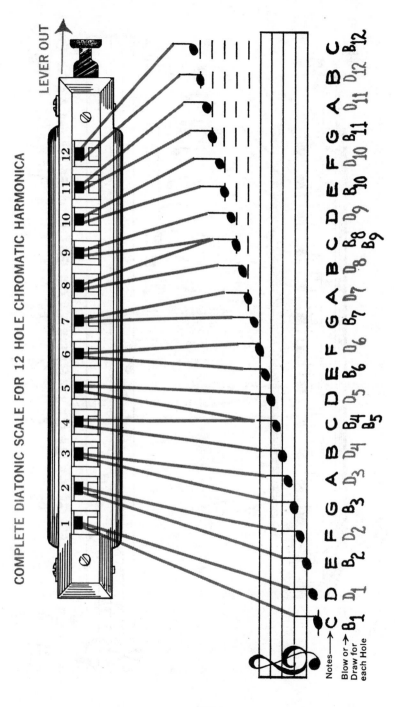

COMPLETE DIATONIC SCALE FOR 12 HOLE CHROMATIC HARMONICA WITH SHARPS

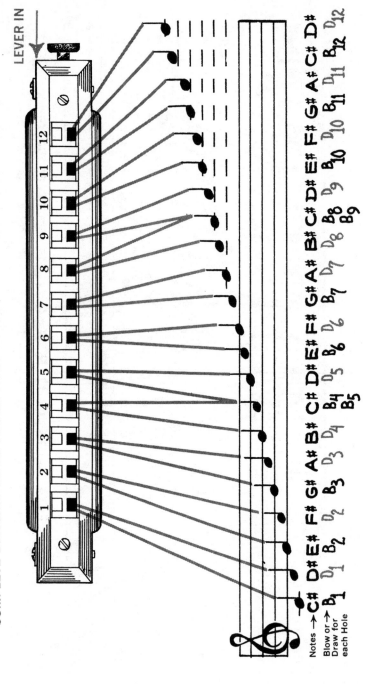

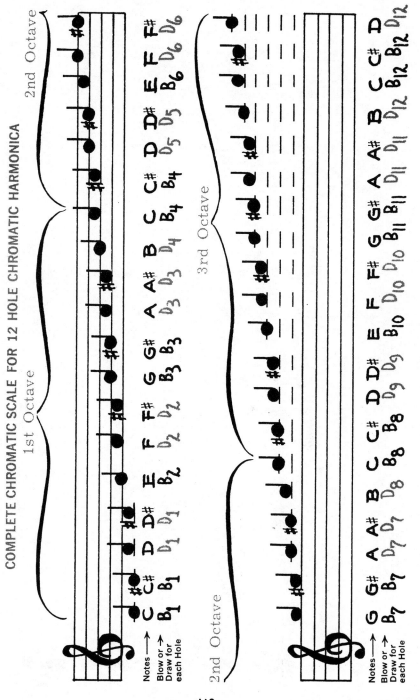

COMPLETE CHROMATIC SCALE FOR 12 HOLE CHROMATIC HARMONICA

113

Points to Remember

1. The 12-Hole, Chromatic Harmonica is almost like the 10-Hole Chromatic with the exception that the former has a range of three complete, chromatic octaves.

2. Practice your chromatic scales until you can play them without thinking.

3. By this time your tonal quality should be excellent.

4. REMEMBER - the musical numbers on your 12-Hole Chromatic are the same as they are on your 10-Hole Chromatic Harmonica.

SANTA LUCIA

O MOON WHOSE MYS-TIC VEIL FROM THE SKY

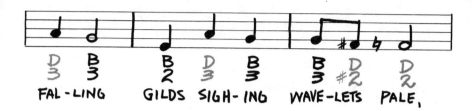

FAL-LING GILDS SIGH-ING WAVE-LETS PALE,

TO OUR HEARTS CALL-ING GLOR-IOUS THE

SUM-MER NIGHT, SEA STRAND AND BIL-LOWS WHITE,

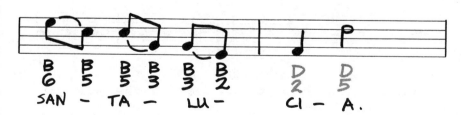

SAN - TA - LU- CI - A.

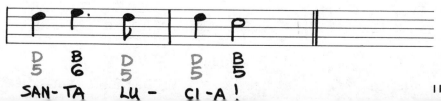

SAN-TA LU - CI-A!

THE BAND PLAYED ON

CA-SEY WOULD WALTZ WITH A STRAW-BER-RY

BLONDE, AND THE BAND PLAYED ON. HE'D

GLIDE O'ER THE FLOOR WITH THE GAL HE A-DORED AND THE

BAND PLAYED ON BUT HIS BRAIN WAS SO

LOAD-ED IT NEAR-LY EX-PLOD-ED. THE POOR GAL WAS

FILLED WITH A-LARM. HE'D NE'ER LEAVE THE

116

GIRL WITH THE STRAW-BER-RY CURL, AND THE

BAND PLAYED ON!

OVER THE WAVES

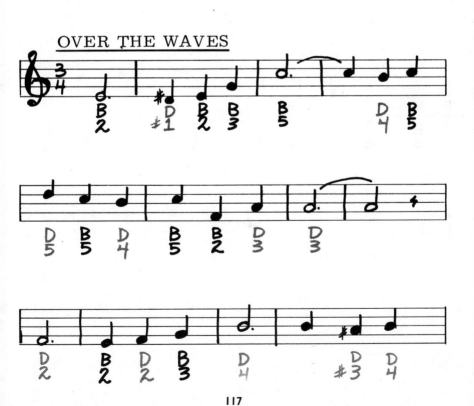

LESSON FIFTEEN

Building Your Image
As A Performer

When you are invited to play at any function whether it be in a private home or public place, be sure you make the best impression possible. No audience, no matter how small or large, should ever be taken for granted. In other words, whether you perform gratis or for a fee, give your very best. Create an image of yourself as a performer that is unique, DON'T IMITATE others. Be gracious in presenting your repertoire. Be modest in taking your bows. Keep a smile in your eyes and on your lips all the time you are before "the public". Unless you have an extensive repertoire, DO NOT ask for requests from your audience. When "the one song" you DON'T know is requested it can be very embarrassing and discouraging. Continued appearances before the public will build your self - confidence and before you know it you will be doing all the correct things without hesitation.

When you perform as a soloist stand up. Sitting and playing do not go together. When you sit you cannot breathe properly and this will hamper your playing. Avoid standing in awkward positions. Assume a natural pose, one that is not too rigid. Sway your body slightly in time with the music. This will create an air of self-confidence in your playing and make your audience more receptive to your music.

Tilt your head slightly to the right. This will eliminate the straight rigid line of your body. Avoid loud stamping or tapping of your foot while keeping time to the song you are playing. The sound will become monotonous and distracting to your listeners. In any performance avoid monotony by varying the tempo of the songs you play. Above all, do NOT repeat long choruses of songs. Keep your music bright and spirited. Trick effects when well done always fascinate your listeners. Always try to convey to your audience that you enjoy playing and that they are being very kind to favor you with their attention. A short, snappy tune for your opening number is an excellent choice for "getting the ear" of your audience. This can be followed by a popular medley, a song of slower tempo or a novelty selection. Always close with a "sure-fire", popular song that "leaves your audience humming".

Announce your numbers in a clear voice. Your choice of songs is very important since they must sustain the interest of your audience. Ease and self-assurance in playing must be acquired. Practice in front of a mirror so that you can "check" any awkwardness in your "style". Remember to let your listeners be the judge of whether or not they want to hear more. No matter how tempted you are to play "just one more number" ... DON'T! The one formula that guarantees the success of any performer is ... ALWAYS LEAVE YOUR AUDIENCE HUNGRY FOR MORE!

A PERSONAL WORD FROM MELVIN POWERS
PUBLISHER, WILSHIRE BOOK COMPANY

Dear Friend:

My goal is to publish interesting, informative, and inspirational books. You can help me accomplish this by answering the following questions, either by phone or by mail. Or, if convenient for you, I would welcome the opportunity to visit with you in my office and hear your comments in person.

Did you enjoy reading this book? Why?

Would you enjoy reading another similar book?

What idea in the book impressed you the most?

If applicable to your situation, have you incorporated this idea in your daily life?

Is there a chapter that could serve as a theme for an entire book? Please explain.

If you have an idea for a book, I would welcome discussing it with you. If you already have one in progress, write or call me concerning possible publication. I can be reached at (213) 875-1711 or (213) 983-1105.

Sincerely yours,

MELVIN POWERS

12015 Sherman Road
North Hollywood, California 91605

MELVIN POWERS SELF-IMPROVEMENT LIBRARY

ASTROLOGY

_____ASTROLOGY: A FASCINATING HISTORY *P. Naylor*	2.00
_____ASTROLOGY: HOW TO CHART YOUR HOROSCOPE *Max Heindel*	3.00
_____ASTROLOGY: YOUR PERSONAL SUN-SIGN GUIDE *Beatrice Ryder*	3.00
_____ASTROLOGY FOR EVERYDAY LIVING *Janet Harris*	2.00
_____ASTROLOGY MADE EASY *Astarte*	2.00
_____ASTROLOGY MADE PRACTICAL *Alexandra Kayhle*	3.00
_____ASTROLOGY, ROMANCE, YOU AND THE STARS *Anthony Norvell*	4.00
_____MY WORLD OF ASTROLOGY *Sydney Omarr*	4.00
_____THOUGHT DIAL *Sydney Omarr*	3.00
_____ZODIAC REVEALED *Rupert Gleadow*	2.00

BRIDGE

_____BRIDGE BIDDING MADE EASY *Edwin B. Kantar*	5.00
_____BRIDGE CONVENTIONS *Edwin B. Kantar*	4.00
_____BRIDGE HUMOR *Edwin B. Kantar*	3.00
_____COMPETITIVE BIDDING IN MODERN BRIDGE *Edgar Kaplan*	4.00
_____DEFENSIVE BRIDGE PLAY COMPLETE *Edwin B. Kantar*	10.00
_____HOW TO IMPROVE YOUR BRIDGE *Alfred Sheinwold*	2.00
_____INTRODUCTION TO DEFENDER'S PLAY *Edwin B. Kantar*	3.00
_____TEST YOUR BRIDGE PLAY *Edwin B. Kantar*	3.00
_____WINNING DECLARER PLAY *Dorothy Hayden Truscott*	4.00

BUSINESS, STUDY & REFERENCE

_____CONVERSATION MADE EASY *Elliot Russell*	2.00
_____EXAM SECRET *Dennis B. Jackson*	2.00
_____FIX-IT BOOK *Arthur Symons*	2.00
_____HOW TO DEVELOP A BETTER SPEAKING VOICE *M. Hellier*	2.00
_____HOW TO MAKE A FORTUNE IN REAL ESTATE *Albert Winnikoff*	3.00
_____INCREASE YOUR LEARNING POWER *Geoffrey A. Dudley*	2.00
_____MAGIC OF NUMBERS *Robert Tocquet*	2.00
_____PRACTICAL GUIDE TO BETTER CONCENTRATION *Melvin Powers*	2.00
_____PRACTICAL GUIDE TO PUBLIC SPEAKING *Maurice Forley*	3.00
_____7 DAYS TO FASTER READING *William S. Schaill*	3.00
_____SONGWRITERS RHYMING DICTIONARY *Jane Shaw Whitfield*	5.00
_____SPELLING MADE EASY *Lester D. Basch & Dr. Milton Finkelstein*	2.00
_____STUDENT'S GUIDE TO BETTER GRADES *J. A. Rickard*	2.00
_____TEST YOURSELF—Find Your Hidden Talent *Jack Shafer*	2.00
_____YOUR WILL & WHAT TO DO ABOUT IT *Attorney Samuel G. Kling*	3.00

CALLIGRAPHY

_____CALLIGRAPHY—The Art of Beautfiul Writing *Katherine Jeffares*	5.00

CHESS & CHECKERS

_____BEGINNER'S GUIDE TO WINNING CHESS *Fred Reinfeld*	3.00
_____BETTER CHESS—How to Play *Fred Reinfeld*	2.00
_____CHECKERS MADE EASY *Tom Wiswell*	2.00
_____CHESS IN TEN EASY LESSONS *Larry Evans*	2.00
_____CHESS MADE EASY *Milton L. Hanauer*	2.00
_____CHESS MASTERY—A New Approach *Fred Reinfeld*	2.00
_____CHESS PROBLEMS FOR BEGINNERS *edited by Fred Reinfeld*	2.00
_____CHESS SECRETS REVEALED *Fred Reinfeld*	2.00
_____CHESS STRATEGY—An Expert's Guide *Fred Reinfeld*	2.00
_____CHESS TACTICS FOR BEGINNERS *edited by Fred Reinfeld*	2.00
_____CHESS THEORY & PRACTICE *Morry & Mitchell*	2.00
_____HOW TO WIN AT CHECKERS *Fred Reinfeld*	2.00
_____1001 BRILLIANT WAYS TO CHECKMATE *Fred Reinfeld*	3.00
_____1001 WINNING CHESS SACRIFICES & COMBINATIONS *Fred Reinfeld*	3.00
_____SOVIET CHESS *Edited by R. G. Wade*	3.00

COOKERY & HERBS

_____CULPEPER'S HERBAL REMEDIES *Dr. Nicholas Culpeper*	2.00
_____FAST GOURMET COOKBOOK *Poppy Cannon*	2.50

_____HEALING POWER OF HERBS *May Bethel* 3.00
_____HERB HANDBOOK *Dawn MacLeod* 2.00
_____HERBS FOR COOKING AND HEALING *Dr. Donald Law* 2.00
_____HERBS FOR HEALTH—How to Grow & Use Them *Louise Evans Doole* 2.00
_____HOME GARDEN COOKBOOK—Delicious Natural Food Recipes *Ken Kraft* 3.00
_____MEDICAL HERBALIST *edited by Dr. J. R. Yemm* 3.00
_____NATURAL FOOD COOKBOOK *Dr. Harry C. Bond* 3.00
_____NATURE'S MEDICINES *Richard Lucas* 3.00
_____VEGETABLE GARDENING FOR BEGINNERS *Hugh Wiberg* 2.00
_____VEGETABLES FOR TODAY'S GARDENS *R. Milton Carleton* 2.00
_____VEGETARIAN COOKERY *Janet Walker* 3.00
_____VEGETARIAN COOKING MADE EASY & DELECTABLE *Veronica Vezza* 2.00
_____VEGETARIAN DELIGHTS—A Happy Cookbook for Health *K. R. Mehta* 2.00
_____VEGETARIAN GOURMET COOKBOOK *Joyce McKinnel* 2.00

GAMBLING & POKER

_____ADVANCED POKER STRATEGY & WINNING PLAY *A. D. Livingston* 3.00
_____HOW NOT TO LOSE AT POKER *Jeffrey Lloyd Castle* 3.00
_____HOW TO WIN AT DICE GAMES *Skip Frey* 3.00
_____HOW TO WIN AT POKER *Terence Reese & Anthony T. Watkins* 2.00
_____SECRETS OF WINNING POKER *George S. Coffin* 3.00
_____WINNING AT CRAPS *Dr. Lloyd T. Commins* 2.00
_____WINNING AT GIN *Chester Wander & Cy Rice* 3.00
_____WINNING AT 21—An Expert's Guide *John Archer* 3.00
_____WINNING POKER SYSTEMS *Norman Zadeh* 3.00

HEALTH

_____DR. LINDNER'S SPECIAL WEIGHT CONTROL METHOD 1.50
_____HELP YOURSELF TO BETTER SIGHT *Margaret Darst Corbett* 3.00
_____HOW TO IMPROVE YOUR VISION *Dr. Robert A. Kraskin* 2.00
_____HOW YOU CAN STOP SMOKING PERMANENTLY *Ernest Caldwell* 2.00
_____MIND OVER PLATTER *Peter G. Lindner, M.D.* 2.00
_____NATURE'S WAY TO NUTRITION & VIBRANT HEALTH *Robert J. Scrutton* 3.00
_____NEW CARBOHYDRATE DIET COUNTER *Patti Lopez-Pereira* 1.50
_____PSYCHEDELIC ECSTASY *William Marshall & Gilbert W. Taylor* 2.00
_____REFLEXOLOGY *Dr. Maybelle Segal* 2.00
_____YOU CAN LEARN TO RELAX *Dr. Samuel Gutwirth* 2.00
_____YOUR ALLERGY—What To Do About It *Allan Knight, M.D.* 2.00

HOBBIES

_____BATON TWIRLING—A Complete Illustrated Guide *Doris Wheelus* 4.00
_____BEACHCOMBING FOR BEGINNERS *Norman Hickin* 2.00
_____BLACKSTONE'S MODERN CARD TRICKS *Harry Blackstone* 2.00
_____BLACKSTONE'S SECRETS OF MAGIC *Harry Blackstone* 2.00
_____BUTTERFLIES 2.50
_____COIN COLLECTING FOR BEGINNERS *Burton Hobson & Fred Reinfeld* 2.00
_____ENTERTAINING WITH ESP *Tony 'Doc' Shiels* 2.00
_____400 FASCINATING MAGIC TRICKS YOU CAN DO *Howard Thurston* 3.00
_____GOULD'S GOLD & SILVER GUIDE TO COINS *Maurice Gould* 2.00
_____HOW I TURN JUNK INTO FUN AND PROFIT *Sari* 3.00
_____HOW TO PLAY THE HARMONICA FOR FUN AND PROFIT *Hal Leighton* 3.00
_____HOW TO WRITE A HIT SONG & SELL IT *Tommy Boyce* 7.00
_____JUGGLING MADE EASY *Rudolf Dittrich* 2.00
_____MAGIC MADE EASY *Byron Wels* 2.00
_____SEW SIMPLY, SEW RIGHT *Mini Rhea & F. Leighton* 2.00
_____STAMP COLLECTING FOR BEGINNERS *Burton Hobson* 2.00
_____STAMP COLLECTING FOR FUN & PROFIT *Frank Cetin* 2.00

HORSE PLAYERS' WINNING GUIDES

_____BETTING HORSES TO WIN *Les Conklin* 3.00
_____ELIMINATE THE LOSERS *Bob McKnight* 3.00
_____HOW TO PICK WINNING HORSES *Bob McKnight* 3.00
_____HOW TO WIN AT THE RACES *Sam (The Genius) Lewin* 3.00
_____HOW YOU CAN BEAT THE RACES *Jack Kavanagh* 3.00

_____SEXUALLY ADEQUATE MALE *Frank S. Caprio, M.D.*   3.00

METAPHYSICS & OCCULT

_____BOOK OF TALISMANS, AMULETS & ZODIACAL GEMS *William Pavitt*   4.00
_____CONCENTRATION—A Guide to Mental Mastery *Mouni Sadhu*   3.00
_____CRITIQUES OF GOD *Edited by Peter Angeles*   7.00
_____DREAMS & OMENS REVEALED *Fred Gettings*   2.00
_____EXTRASENSORY PERCEPTION *Simeon Edmunds*   2.00
_____EXTRA-TERRESTRIAL INTELLIGENCE—The First Encounter   6.00
_____FORTUNE TELLING WITH CARDS *P. Foli*   2.00
_____HANDWRITING ANALYSIS MADE EASY *John Marley*   2.00
_____HANDWRITING TELLS *Nadya Olyanova*   3.00
_____HOW TO UNDERSTAND YOUR DREAMS *Geoffrey A. Dudley*   2.00
_____ILLUSTRATED YOGA *William Zorn*   3.00
_____IN DAYS OF GREAT PEACE *Mouni Sadhu*   3.00
_____KING SOLOMON'S TEMPLE IN THE MASONIC TRADITION *Alex Horne*   5.00
_____LSD—THE AGE OF MIND *Bernard Roseman*   2.00
_____MAGICIAN—His training and work *W. E. Butler*   2.00
_____MEDITATION *Mouni Sadhu*   4.00
_____MODERN NUMEROLOGY *Morris C. Goodman*   3.00
_____NUMEROLOGY—ITS FACTS AND SECRETS *Ariel Yvon Taylor*   2.00
_____PALMISTRY MADE EASY *Fred Gettings*   2.00
_____PALMISTRY MADE PRACTICAL *Elizabeth Daniels Squire*   3.00
_____PALMISTRY SECRETS REVEALED *Henry Frith*   2.00
_____PRACTICAL YOGA *Ernest Wood*   3.00
_____PROPHECY IN OUR TIME *Martin Ebon*   2.50
_____PSYCHOLOGY OF HANDWRITING *Nadya Olyanova*   3.00
_____SEEING INTO THE FUTURE *Harvey Day*   2.00
_____SUPERSTITION—Are you superstitious? *Eric Maple*   2.00
_____TAROT *Mouni Sadhu*   4.00
_____TAROT OF THE BOHEMIANS *Papus*   5.00
_____TEST YOUR ESP *Martin Ebon*   2.00
_____WAYS TO SELF-REALIZATION *Mouni Sadhu*   3.00
_____WITCHCRAFT, MAGIC & OCCULTISM—A Fascinating History *W. B. Crow* 3.00
_____WITCHCRAFT—THE SIXTH SENSE *Justine Glass*   2.00
_____WORLD OF PSYCHIC RESEARCH *Hereward Carrington*   2.00
_____YOU CAN ANALYZE HANDWRITING *Robert Holder*   2.00

SELF-HELP & INSPIRATIONAL

_____CYBERNETICS WITHIN US *Y. Saparina*   3.00
_____DAILY POWER FOR JOYFUL LIVING *Dr. Donald Curtis*   2.00
_____DOCTOR PSYCHO-CYBERNETICS *Maxwell Maltz, M.D.*   3.00
_____DYNAMIC THINKING *Melvin Powers*   2.00
_____EXUBERANCE—Your Guide to Happiness & Fulfillment *Dr. Paul Kurtz* 3.00
_____GREATEST POWER IN THE UNIVERSE *U. S. Andersen*   4.00
_____GROW RICH WHILE YOU SLEEP *Ben Sweetland*   3.00
_____GROWTH THROUGH REASON *Albert Ellis, Ph.D.*   3.00
_____GUIDE TO DEVELOPING YOUR POTENTIAL *Herbert A. Otto, Ph.D.*   3.00
_____GUIDE TO LIVING IN BALANCE *Frank S. Caprio, M.D.*   2.00
_____HELPING YOURSELF WITH APPLIED PSYCHOLOGY *R. Henderson*   2.00
_____HELPING YOURSELF WITH PSYCHIATRY *Frank S. Caprio, M.D.*   2.00
_____HOW TO ATTRACT GOOD LUCK *A. H. Z. Carr*   3.00
_____HOW TO CONTROL YOUR DESTINY *Norvell*   3.00
_____HOW TO DEVELOP A WINNING PERSONALITY *Martin Panzer*   3.00
_____HOW TO DEVELOP AN EXCEPTIONAL MEMORY *Young & Gibson*   4.00
_____HOW TO OVERCOME YOUR FEARS *M. P. Leahy, M.D.*   2.00
_____HOW YOU CAN HAVE CONFIDENCE AND POWER *Les Giblin*   3.00
_____HUMAN PROBLEMS & HOW TO SOLVE THEM *Dr. Donald Curtis*   3.00
_____I CAN *Ben Sweetland*   4.00
_____I WILL *Ben Sweetland*   3.00
_____LEFT-HANDED PEOPLE *Michael Barsley*   3.00
_____MAGIC IN YOUR MIND *U. S. Andersen*   3.00

_____MAGIC OF THINKING BIG *Dr. David J. Schwartz* 3.00
_____MAGIC POWER OF YOUR MIND *Walter M. Germain* 4.00
_____MENTAL POWER THROUGH SLEEP SUGGESTION *Melvin Powers* 2.00
_____NEW GUIDE TO RATIONAL LIVING *Albert Ellis, Ph.D. & R. Harper, Ph.D.* 3.00
_____OUR TROUBLED SELVES *Dr. Allan Fromme* 3.00
_____PRACTICAL GUIDE TO SUCCESS & POPULARITY *C. W. Bailey* 2.00
_____PSYCHO-CYBERNETICS *Maxwell Maltz, M.D.* 2.00
_____SCIENCE OF MIND IN DAILY LIVING *Dr. Donald Curtis* 2.00
_____SECRET POWER OF THE PYRAMIDS *U. S. Andersen* 4.00
_____SECRET OF SECRETS *U. S. Andersen* 4.00
_____STUTTERING AND WHAT YOU CAN DO ABOUT IT *W. Johnson, Ph.D.* 2.50
_____SUCCESS-CYBERNETICS *U. S. Andersen* 4.00
_____10 DAYS TO A GREAT NEW LIFE *William E. Edwards* 3.00
_____THINK AND GROW RICH *Napoleon Hill* 3.00
_____THREE MAGIC WORDS *U. S. Andersen* 4.00
_____TREASURY OF THE ART OF LIVING *Sidney S. Greenberg* 5.00
_____YOU ARE NOT THE TARGET *Laura Huxley* 3.00
_____YOUR SUBCONSCIOUS POWER *Charles M. Simmons* 4.00
_____YOUR THOUGHTS CAN CHANGE YOUR LIFE *Dr. Donald Curtis* 3.00

SPORTS
_____ARCHERY—An Expert's Guide *Dan Stamp* 2.00
_____BICYCLING FOR FUN AND GOOD HEALTH *Kenneth E. Luther* 2.00
_____BILLIARDS—Pocket • Carom • Three Cushion *Clive Cottingham, Jr.* 2.00
_____CAMPING-OUT 101 Ideas & Activities *Bruno Knobel* 2.00
_____COMPLETE GUIDE TO FISHING *Vlad Evanoff* 2.00
_____HOW TO WIN AT POCKET BILLIARDS *Edward D. Knuchell* 3.00
_____LEARNING & TEACHING SOCCER SKILLS *Eric Worthington* 3.00
_____MOTORCYCLING FOR BEGINNERS *I. G. Edmonds* 2.00
_____PRACTICAL BOATING *W. S. Kals* 3.00
_____SECRET OF BOWLING STRIKES *Dawson Taylor* 2.00
_____SECRET OF PERFECT PUTTING *Horton Smith & Dawson Taylor* 3.00
_____SECRET WHY FISH BITE *James Westman* 2.00
_____SKIER'S POCKET BOOK *Otti Wiedman* (4¼" x 6") 2.50
_____SOCCER—The game & how to play it *Gary Rosenthal* 2.00
_____STARTING SOCCER *Edward F. Dolan, Jr.* 2.00
_____TABLE TENNIS MADE EASY *Johnny Leach* 2.00

TENNIS LOVERS' LIBRARY
_____BEGINNER'S GUIDE TO WINNING TENNIS *Helen Hull Jacobs* 2.00
_____HOW TO BEAT BETTER TENNIS PLAYERS *Loring Fiske* 4.00
_____HOW TO IMPROVE YOUR TENNIS—Style, Strategy & Analysis *C. Wilson* 2.00
_____INSIDE TENNIS—Techniques of Winning *Jim Leighton* 3.00
_____PLAY TENNIS WITH ROSEWALL *Ken Rosewall* 2.00
_____PSYCH YOURSELF TO BETTER TENNIS *Dr. Walter A. Luszki* 2.00
_____SUCCESSFUL TENNIS *Neale Fraser* 2.00
_____TENNIS FOR BEGINNERS *Dr. H. A. Murray* 2.00
_____TENNIS MADE EASY *Joel Brecheen* 2.00
_____WEEKEND TENNIS—How to have fun & win at the same time *Bill Talbert* 3.00
_____WINNING WITH PERCENTAGE TENNIS—Smart Strategy *Jack Lowe* 2.00

WILSHIRE PET LIBRARY
_____DOG OBEDIENCE TRAINING *Gust Kessopulos* 3.00
_____DOG TRAINING MADE EASY & FUN *John W. Kellogg* 2.00
_____HOW TO BRING UP YOUR PET DOG *Kurt Unkelbach* 2.00
_____HOW TO RAISE & TRAIN YOUR PUPPY *Jeff Griffen* 2.00
_____PIGEONS: HOW TO RAISE & TRAIN THEM *William H. Allen, Jr.* 2.00

*The books listed above can be obtained from your book dealer or directly from
Melvin Powers. When ordering, please remit 25c per book postage & handling.
Send for our free illustrated catalog of self-improvement books.*

Melvin Powers
12015 Sherman Road, No. Hollywood, California 91605